AZTECS
AND INCAS

© Aladdin Books Ltd 1988

Designed and produced by
Aladdin Books Ltd
70 Old Compton Street
London W1

First published in the
United States in 1988 by
Franklin Watts
387 Park Avenue South
New York, NY 10016

ISBN 0 531 10622 5

Library of Congress Catalog
Card Number: 88-50497

Printed in Belgium

Design   David West
             Children's Book Design

Editor   Denny Robson

Researcher   Cecilia Weston-Baker

Illustrator Rob Shone

Consultant   Elizabeth Carmichael,
             Assistant Keeper,
             Museum of Mankind,
             London.

CONTENTS

GREAT CIVILIZATIONS

AZTECS AND INCAS
AD 1300-1532

Penny Bateman

FRANKLIN WATTS
New York·London·Toronto·Sydney

INTRODUCTION

More than 30,000 years ago, the first people to settle in the Americas crossed over from Asia to the land which is now called Alaska. Over thousands of years more people arrived and different groups traveled south, settling in all parts of the two continents.

Over 500 years ago, there were many different groups of people living in North and South America. Some were hunters, but most were farmers. Some lived in towns and cities. Two of these groups, the Aztecs and the Incas, became rulers of great empires. The Aztecs controlled many different peoples in Mexico and parts of Central America. The vast empire of the Inca covered the land which is now the modern countries of Peru, Bolivia, Ecuador and part of Chile. The Aztec and Inca empires were thousands of miles apart, separated by mountains, rain forests and sea. They both had enormous power for about 100 years until they were conquered by the Spanish in the early 1500s.

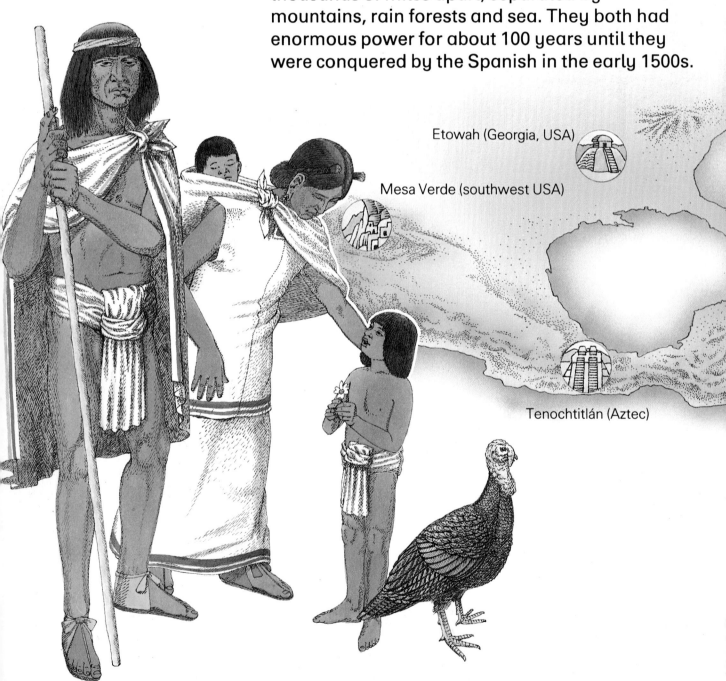

Etowah (Georgia, USA)

Mesa Verde (southwest USA)

Tenochtitlán (Aztec)

Although much of the Aztec and Inca civilizations was destroyed by the Spanish, we know a great deal about their way of life. This is because there are still remains of Aztec and Inca buildings, pottery, jewelry, books and other objects that we can look at today and study. We also have the records of the Spanish invaders who described what they saw.

This book looks first at the history of the Aztecs, where they came from, how they lived and how this small group of hunters and farmers eventually came to have a large empire. The second part of the book looks at the Inca people who successfully ruled over one of the most mountainous lands in the world.

The picture shows an Aztec family (left) and an Inca family (right). On the map are just some of the bigger places where people lived at the same time the Aztecs were in Mexico and the Incas in Peru. Today the descendants of these original Americans still live in North and South America.

Machu Picchu
(Inca)

Tupinamba
towns (Brazil

GROWTH OF AN EMPIRE AD 1300-1486

The Aztecs believed their ancestors were hunting people who lived in northern Mexico. Long ago they set out to find a better home. For many years they wandered, until their god Huitzilopochtli guided them to the Valley of Mexico and Lake Texcoco about 1300 AD. Other peoples had been living in this area for thousands of years and there were already many towns around the lake shore.

For a time, the Aztecs worked for some of the rulers of these towns. But finally they moved onto the marshy islands of the lake, the only land other people did not want. They began to reclaim the land. They fished, farmed and built a settlement of reed houses with a temple for their god. They eventually united with other peoples on the shore. They were then strong enough to defeat the most powerful people in the area, the Azcapotzalcos. They claimed their land. This was the beginning of the Aztec empire.

A god's prophecy

The Aztecs believed the god Huitzilopochtli told them to find the spot where an eagle stood on a cactus holding a snake. It was here they would build a city and become great rulers. The eagle was said to have been found on one of the islands of Lake Texcoco as prophesied. It was here the Aztec city of Tenochtitlán was built.

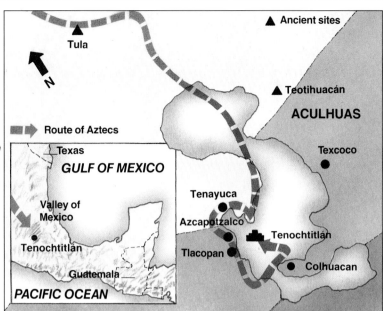

Datechart

c30,000 BC People from Asia begin to cross into the Americas to the land now called Alaska.

c1200-400 BC One of the first great civilizations in Mexico is the Olmec. Many ideas used by later peoples are developed by them.

AD 100-600 The first major city in the Valley of Mexico, near Lake Texcoco, is Teotihuacán. At its greatest, over 150,000 people live there.

AD 900-1200 A people called the Toltecs rule from their city Tula in the Valley of Mexico. The Aztecs believed they were great artists and called their own craftspeople *toltecas*.

AD 1100-1300 The Aztecs spend many years wandering in northern Mexico.

AD 1200-1323 Among the different peoples the Aztecs work for at this time are the Colhuacan. But they drive out the Aztecs when the Aztecs sacrifice a Colhuacan princess.

AD 1345 The Aztecs found their city Tenochtitlán, meaning place of the prickly pear cactus.

AD 1419 Nezahualcoyotl becomes ruler of the neighboring kingdom, Texcoco. It is one of the centers for arts and sciences in Mexico. It influences the Aztecs and other peoples. The Texcocan ruler himself is a famous poet.

AD 1428 The Aztecs defeat Azcapotzalco.

AD 1440-68 The ruler Motecuhzoma expands the empire to the coast of the Gulf of Mexico.

Aztec beginnings

Long before the time of the Aztecs, there had been other powerful states in Mexico. The Aztecs visited some of their ruined cities to worship at the ancient temples. The Aztecs admired and copied their style of architecture, art and religion.

The capital of an empire

Tenochtitlán (above and center) was slowly built on reclaimed land. As the city increased in size, there was a greater demand for materials not found on the lake. So the Aztecs fought to conquer new lands.

The Aztec army was feared throughout Mexico. Aztec warriors fought fiercely. Success meant they would be rewarded with gifts of slaves, cloth and land. The more prisoners a soldier took, the higher the rank he was given. Different ranks were shown by different styles of costumes, shown below.

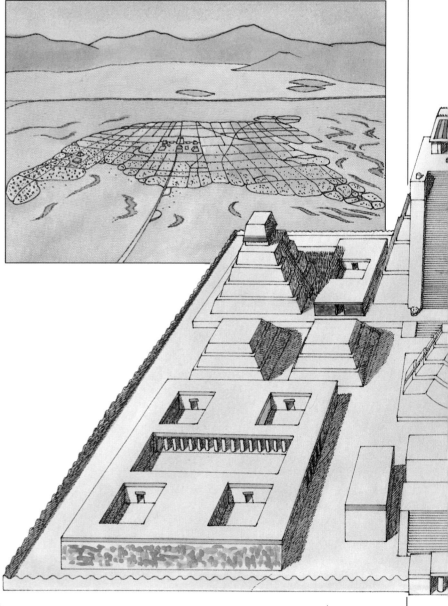

Gods and beliefs

The Aztecs believed the world had been destroyed four times. The fifth world in which they lived began when their gods sacrificed themselves to create the sun. In order to thank the gods and to help the sun in its nightly battle with the moon and stars, the Aztecs gave offerings of many kinds. The most important gift they had was human blood. In wars they captured people for sacrifice. Without this food for the gods the Aztecs thought the world would end.

There were hundreds of gods. Some, like the rain god Tlaloc, were important to all people. Other gods were special only for certain groups, such as artists or merchants. There were many religious ceremonies. A few still survive today, like the performance of *voladores* shown in the photograph in which fliers circle a pole.

The emperor

When the Aztecs were a small band of people the heads of each family made decisions together. As the empire grew, the most important people in the government, army and religion elected an emperor to rule.

People had to treat the emperor with great respect. He relied on a group of advisers to help him rule. The most important of these was called Snake-Woman. An Aztec emperor was expected to look after the welfare of his people. Emperor Motecuhzoma I gave food and clothing to the whole population. Emperor Ahuitzotl gave corn to flood victims.

Life in the country

Most people in the empire were peasant farmers. The whole family worked long hours together to grow, store and prepare the food they needed.

Aztec farmers were commoners. They had certain rights protected by law. In return they paid taxes in the form of food and clothing. Men could be made to fight and work on public projects.

Food for an empire

The whole empire depended on farming. The main food crop was corn, but other common vegetables were beans, squashes and chili peppers. The Aztecs kept turkeys, small dogs and ducks, as well as rabbits and bees for food.

The nobles

Aztec people were either nobles, common people, slaves, or they belonged to a special group such as craftspeople or merchants. A man became a noble because he had an important government job or because he was a priest or a high-ranking warrior. A woman was usually a noble if her family or husband was, but she could own property and run a business in her own right. Nobles were expected to do their work well. In return they received fine houses and servants and could afford to entertain with lavish banquets.

The market in Tenochtitlán had everything from precious stones to vegetables. Over 60,000 people sold their produce there at one time.

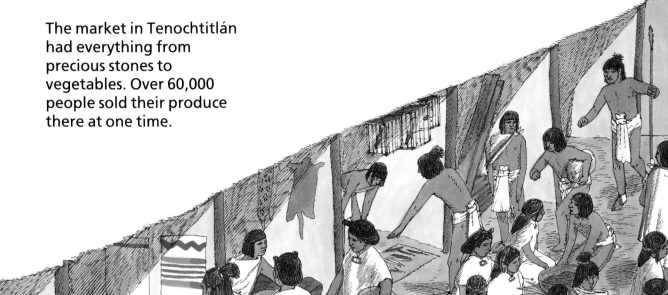

By the time Motecuhzoma II became ruler in 1502, the empire had become the largest it would ever be. It included millions of people in many different cities and states. These defeated states were ruled by leaders loyal to the Aztec emperor. They had to give goods to the emperor who sent ambassadors to act on his behalf and send back news. Many people were unhappy under the control of the Aztecs and there were many revolts. The army was used to stop these and to defend the empire against its enemies.

At the empire's center was Tenochtitlán, which had become a rich city of over half a million people. It had towering stone temples, beautiful public buildings, palaces for the rich and sprawling suburbs of houses. There were zoos and beautiful gardens. Streets would be full of people from all over the empire, some on government business, others bringing goods to market and others leaving for distant lands.

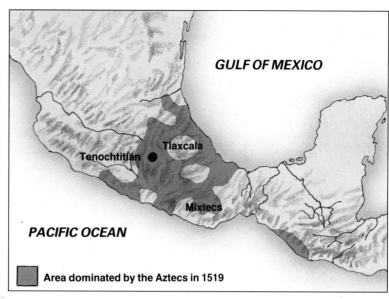

GULF OF MEXICO

Tlaxcala

Tenochtitlán

Mixtecs

PACIFIC OCEAN

Area dominated by the Aztecs in 1519

Datechart

AD 1486-1502 Ahuizotl expands the Aztec empire as far as the Pacific coast and the borders of present-day Guatemala.

AD 1500 Tenochtitlán is flooded. Crops are destroyed and many people drown. Many houses have to be rebuilt including the emperor's palace.

AD 1502 Motecuhzoma II becomes emperor at the age of 32.

AD 1504 War breaks out between the Aztecs and the Tlaxcalans whose land is completely surrounded by the Aztec empire. The fighting continues for many years supplying both sides with prisoners for sacrifice.

AD1507 A New Fire Ceremony takes place. At the end of each 52 year period, all fires are put out. A new fire is built on the chest of a sacrificed prisoner. If it does not take, it is thought the world will end. It is with relief the Aztecs see the flames and torches are carried to all parts of the capital to light other fires. A new period has begun.

AD 1519 (spring) Hernán Cortés and 600 Spanish land on the shore of Mexico.

AD 1519 (summer) The Spanish defeat the Tlaxcalans who become their allies against the Aztec.

AD 1520 The Spanish invaders kill many people celebrating a festival. The Aztecs rise up and drive the Spanish out of the city. Emperor Motecuhzoma II is killed.

AD 1521 The Spanish and their allies beseige Tenochtitlán for 80 days and finally defeat the Aztecs.

THE EMPIRE AT ITS HEIGHT

Merchants and spies

Under cover of darkness, lines of men loaded down with heavy packs would quietly enter the city. These were merchants and their porters returning from distant lands bringing back luxuries and other goods. Merchants were a special group of people with their own gods, laws, and customs. Trading trips could last years. They were often very dangerous but they could also be very profitable.

Some important areas for trade were the tropical lands just to the south. Here they got valuable jade, sacred quetzal bird feathers, cocoa beans, jaguar skins and other luxuries. Some merchants disguised themselves as spies to search for new trade routes and to gather information. The merchants took care not to show off their great wealth in case the ruling classes thought they were too powerful.

merchant spy

Aztec art

Artists were greatly respected in Aztec times. Even the children of royalty and nobles were encouraged to take up an art or craft. Each region of the empire had its own specialists. For instance, the Mixtec people were famous for gold and mosaic work.

Finely spun and woven cloth was produced by women. Featherworkers made brilliantly colored costumes. Artists cut and polished jade and turquoise to make religious objects and jewelry. Sculptors made stone and wooden statues for temples. Metalsmiths melted and cast gold for beautiful jewelry, like the Mixtec ornament in the photograph.

Growing up

Aztec parents were very strict with their children. Both boys and girls began to learn the skills they would need as adults at an early age.

Every Aztec boy had to go to school. A commoner's son learned how to be a warrior. A rich person's son might attend a religious school to train as a priest or leader in the government.

There were schools for girls but they were not compulsory. Girls could learn to become priestesses and were taught weaving and embroidery. After a few years most married.

Science and books

The Aztecs were interested in science. Some people were healers. They used both religion and knowledge of herbs to fight illness. Priests studied the stars so they could divide time into years, months and days. They believed that the state of their world depended on performing ceremonies or doing deeds at exactly the right time. The carving on the Aztec stone (photograph below) shows the sun in the center and the signs of the 20 days in an Aztec month.

Writing has been important in Mexico for over two thousand years. The Aztec priests wrote mainly history and religious books. The writing was picture writing. Books were made of folded sheets of bark paper or deerskin.

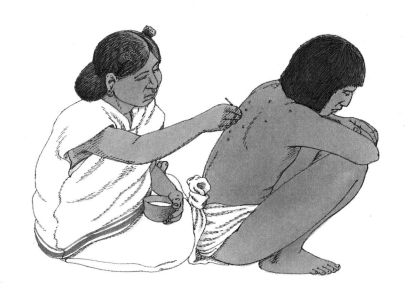

Games

The most popular Aztec gambling game was *patolli*. Colored pebbles were moved according to the throw of marked beans used as dice. Many people became addicted, often gambling all their family's belongings and their land. Some even gambled themselves into slavery.

The ball-game *tlachtli* was important all over Mexico. It was a religious game played during important festivals. It took place in special courts between two teams. To score one team had to get a rubber ball into their opponents' end. They could only touch the ball with their hips and knees. It could be a very rough game and players were often injured or even killed. One way of winning instantly was to get the ball through a stone ring on the wall of the court. The winner could take the clothes of the spectators – if he and his friends could catch them!

GROWTH OF THE INCA EMPIRE

About six or seven hundred years ago, several small groups of people lived in the southern Andes, a mountain range in Peru. They spent much of their time fighting each other and raiding enemy villages. One of these groups was the Incas. Eventually they became the most powerful group. They conquered some neighboring peoples and became a small state, ruled from the capital city of Cuzco.

During the next hundred years, they secured their position by defeating all the enemies in their region. The Incas then turned their forces towards the north, south and finally the powerful peoples on the coast of Peru. After long battles the Incas defeated them all and became the rulers of one of the longest empires in the world. Their empire stretched over 1,850 miles from southern Colombia to central Chile. To control the empire, the Incas built thousands of miles of roads over difficult mountainous land.

Messengers constantly traveled the roads on foot with news from all the major towns. The army used the roads to reach danger areas quickly. Storehouses of food and equipment along the way kept travelers supplied.

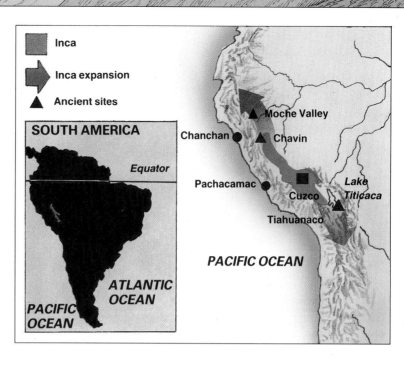

Inca

Inca expansion

Ancient sites

SOUTH AMERICA

Equator

ATLANTIC OCEAN

PACIFIC OCEAN

Moche Valley

Chanchan

Chavin

Pachacamac

Cuzco

Lake Titicaca

Tiahuanaco

PACIFIC OCEAN

Datechart

c18,000 BC People are already living in the area that is now Peru. They are hunters and gatherers of wild food.

c5,500 BC People begin to farm in this area.

c800-600 BC The Chavin are one of the first people to have great influence in Peru. Their religion spreads to many places. Images of their main cat-like god appear in the art of people living hundreds of years after the Chavin disappear.

AD 100-800 Although they had no writing, the Moche people leave a wonderful record of their life and beliefs on their pottery painted with detailed scenes of daily life.

c AD 1200-1470 On the north coast of Peru the kingdom of the Chimu people extends over 600 mi. The capital is Chanchan, a huge city built of mud bricks. When the Inca, with over 30,000 people, defeat the Chimu, they borrow much of their art styles and way of life.

AD 1200 According to legend, the first Inca emperor, Manco Capac, begins his rule. The Inca also found their capital city Cuzco.

AD 1438 The Inca are attacked and almost defeated by a neighboring people, the Chanca. The emperor Viracocha runs away but Cuzco is saved by one of his sons, Yupanqui, who remains and leads the defense.

AD 1471-1493 During Topa Inca's reign the empire reaches Chile.

The people before
The early city state of the Moche of northern Peru (c AD100-800) had impressive pyramids, irrigation systems, pottery (right) and textiles. Many religions, art and building methods began long before the Incas were powerful. The Incas were quick to copy or borrow from the past and the peoples they conquered.

Armies and conquests
Inca expeditions were successful because they had a number of good leaders and a disciplined army. All men trained to fight in case they were needed. The soldiers' weapons were bronze-headed clubs, slings and spears.

The Inca palace

The emperor's palace was a series of government offices, workshops, store rooms and public halls. Royal guards, servants and government administrators lived and worked there, as well as the royal family. This was the center from which the empire was ruled.

The rooms where the emperor and his family lived were like those of poorer people, but on a grander scale. The furniture was sparse and simple. The walls, however, were made of fine stone and often decorated with paint or plaques of gold and silver.

Keeping in touch

Although the Incas did not have a writing system, they had other methods of recording events and keeping government accounts. They used a *quipu*, a special system of knotted and colored strings. These were "read" by trained people called *quipucamayocs*. The Incas also passed on their history and religion through stories, songs and poems.

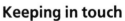

The people of the empire

There were many different peoples in the Inca empire. Each had their own customs, which they were allowed to keep as long as they obeyed the laws of the empire. By law they had to wear their unique styles of costume so that each group could be easily identified.

The Incas believed themselves to be the superior group. True Incas were either people of royal blood or people who had been made Incas as a reward. Incas were easy to identify by their large ear ornaments.

Taxes and welfare

Most people had to pay taxes to the ruler, to the religious leaders and to the local community. Taxes were paid in the form of food, goods such as cloth, and work. Every year each village sent men to the mines, to build roads and public buildings, or to be soldiers. Farmers had to work the fields of the emperor and priests as well as their own lands.

In return there were social benefits. Old people, widows and orphans were cared for. There were storehouses full of goods that were given to people according to their needs and social position.

Keeping control

When a new region was conquered, an Inca of royal blood would be chosen to govern it. Under this ruler, the local leaders were allowed to keep their posts as long as they were loyal to the emperor. By allowing this the Incas believed the conquered people would be less likely to revolt.

Often the defeated leaders' children were taken as hostages to Cuzco. The children would be treated and educated like other nobles. But they were insurance for their fathers' cooperation.

In the same way statues of local gods were brought to Cuzco to prevent rebellions. The Inca would also send whole communities of troublemakers to live in more secure areas, and loyal people were moved to live with newly conquered groups.

INCA SOCIETY AD 1493-1532

By the end of the 15th century, the Inca empire had become a very rich state. Vast quantities of copper, gold and silver were being mined. There were many successful trading expeditions to other parts of South America. The storehouses of the empire were full.

But this wealth had little effect on the majority of the common people. For them life was much the same as before the Incas – except they had to pay more taxes and had less freedom. They were not allowed to travel long distances, wear fine clothing or have riches like gold and silver.

In contrast the nobility became very wealthy. They used gold and silver objects, their clothes were made of the finest wool and cotton, and they wore jewelry of precious metals. They lived in well-built houses with servants to look after them. Commoners could be punished by torture, but a noble would only receive a public warning. A commoner's life had the same value as a noble's honor.

The Inca people believed the emperor, called Sapa Inca, was the descendant of the sun. This gave him the right to rule. When he died, his preserved body was kept in his palace where servants continued to wait on him. On important occasions the mummies of the dead Sapa Incas would be paraded with great honor.

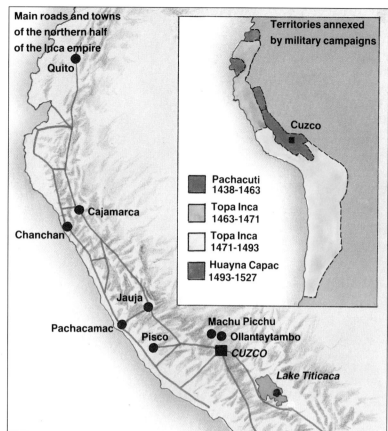

Main roads and towns of the northern half of the Inca empire

Quito

Cajamarca

Chanchan

Jauja

Pachacamac

Pisco

Machu Picchu
Ollantaytambo
CUZCO

Lake Titicaca

Territories annexed by military campaigns

Cuzco

Pachacuti 1438-1463
Topa Inca 1463-1471
Topa Inca 1471-1493
Huayna Capac 1493-1527

Datechart

AD 1493-1527 The emperor Huayna Capac extends the empire as far north as the modern borders of Colombia and Ecuador. During Huayna Capac's reign, an adventurer called Alejo Garcia is the first European to visit the Inca Empire. He travels from Brazil.

AD 1527 Huayna Capac hears that foreigners have been seen on the coast. These are the Spanish led by Francisco Pizarro exploring the region. Soon after, the emperor dies, possibly of smallpox. This disease was brought by the Spanish.

AD 1527 Pizarro captures an Inca ocean-going raft loaded with gold and silver ornaments and other riches for trading.

AD 1527-1532 There is civil war between two rivals for the Inca throne – Huascar and Atahuallpa. The latter finally wins.

AD 1532 (spring) Pizarro leads his soldiers into the Inca empire.

AD 1532 The Spanish capture Atahuallpa. The Incas fill a large room full of gold and a hut twice full of silver to pay for his ransom. Despite this, the Spanish kill him. After his death the Incas still fight back. Many Incas flee into the eastern forests and keep up resistance for several years.

INCA SOCIETY

Running the empire

The population of the Inca empire was organized like a pyramid. At the top was the Sapa Inca. The ordinary people were at the bottom. In between there were leaders responsible for a certain number of taxpayers. The least important leader was in charge of 10 taxpayers, the next 100, and so on. The four most important men below the emperor each governed a quarter of the empire.

This system meant that laws and orders could be passed down through the chain of leaders to the ordinary people. And information about the commoners could be passed up to the Sapa Inca.

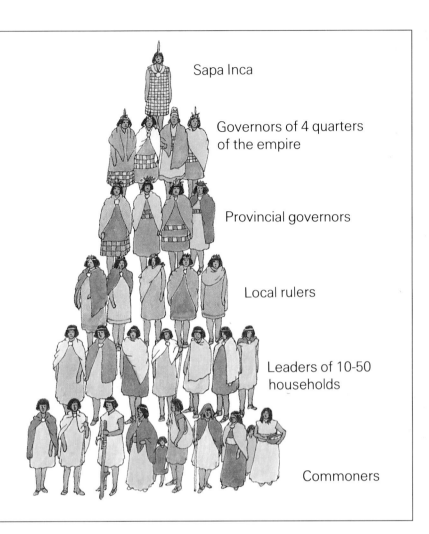

Sapa Inca

Governors of 4 quarters of the empire

Provincial governors

Local rulers

Leaders of 10-50 households

Commoners

Farming

Farmers in the Inca empire helped each other with plowing, planting and harvesting, just as they do in Peru today. In the mountains where the land was steep, they cut terraces to make flat fields. Canals were built to direct water down the slopes to dry areas. A sharp pointed digging stick was used for plowing and planting. It is still used today (photograph right).

Different crops were grown at different heights – tropical fruits and vegetables in the low valleys, grains and some root vegetables higher up.

At home in the mountains

This family is preparing its main meal. The son brings in the fuel. His sister grinds the corn for cakes. A vegetable stew and soup are cooking on the clay stove. Peasant families would eat very little meat as their animals were too valuable to kill frequently for food.

Living in the mountains could be very cold. The house has thick stone walls and a thatched roof. There are no windows and the one room is dark. There is little furniture. As most of the time is spent out of doors there is little need for comfort. On the floor guinea pigs eat scraps, keeping the house clean. They may also be eaten.

Alpacas and llamas were kept

People fished the sea and lakes

INCA SOCIETY

Gods and festivals

The Incas believed the world was created by the god Viracocha. But they thought other gods affected humans most – the gods of the earth and sky. The Incas made offerings of animals and sometimes human sacrifices to them.

All the gods were thought to help increase crops and animal herds. Important religious festivals would be held at the beginning of each growing season. In this picture royalty are taking part in the ceremony of the planting of the first corn. The men make the first holes in the earth and the women follow them planting a few corn seeds. A festival with drink, food and dancing would follow and then the farmers would begin the real planting work.

A woman in power

The Coya, the emperor's wife, had an important role in the running of the empire. She was connected with the female god, the Moon. She sometimes took the place of the ruler in Cuzco when he was away. She also took part in many agricultural ceremonies and had a great interest in nature. Her own gardens were full of different kinds of plants and animals. Here the Coya is shown having her hair combed by her women attendants.

Building in stone

The Incas had excellent engineers and architects. In the picture a clay model is being used to plan a new building. Stonemasons are shaping the blocks for the walls. Stoneworkers used hand tools such as bronze and stone chisels, mallets and crowbars. They cut stone so well that blocks fitted tightly together without mortar.

Many Inca walls are still standing, despite many earthquakes. The stones used were often rounded at the edges or polished to catch the bright light and make patterns. One of the Inca achievements was to build in mountainous areas. The most famous example is Machu Picchu (photograph above), built on a high steep slope.

Art to wear

Beautiful cloth was very valuable to the Incas. The finest cloth was made of the wool of alpaca or its cousin, the wild vicuña, woven by highly trained men and women.

The girls and women shown here are in a special school or convent where they spent much time spinning and weaving. They were selected from all over the empire to be priestesses or wives of nobles or royalty.

THE AZTEC AND INCA LEGACY

The Spanish arrived in Mexico and Peru in the early 1500s. They were amazed by the splendor and sophistication of the cities. They wanted the great riches they found and so they attacked both empires.

They were fiercely resisted but after several years they conquered both empires. Shiploads of gold and silver objects were melted down and sent to Spain. The Aztec and Inca religions were stopped and sacred objects and temples were destroyed. The American peoples had new masters.

CONQVISTA DE MEXICO POR CORTES. 7

The conquerors

The photograph above shows a 17th century painting of the final Spanish attack on Tenochtitlán. Enemies of the Aztecs such as the Tlaxcalans helped the Spanish win.

After both conquests, most people of the old empires were made slaves. Thousands died in wars, or due to overwork or European diseases like smallpox.

Aztec and Inca today

Evidence of Aztec and Inca cultures still survive, such as the Inca walls in Cuzco that support Spanish colonial buildings (top right).

The descendants of the Aztecs and Incas are a living link with the past. Many are trying to improve living conditions and to protect their rights and land. They are proud of their past and many still follow ways of life that can be traced back to before the conquest. The Mexicans in the photograph (center right) are honoring their dead during 'The Day of the Dead' festival. Others take part in a religious procession (bottom right). Both festivals have European and native American origins. And below, Peruvian villagers still hold markets on ancient Inca sites.

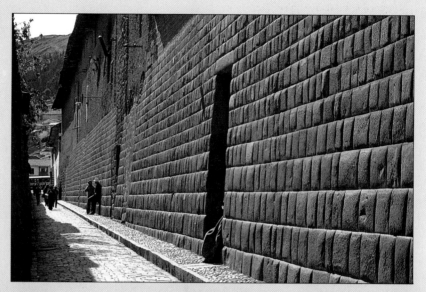

INDEX

Photographic Credits:
Pages 9, 16, 26, 29 and 31 (top, bottom left and bottom right): Hutchison Library; pages 14 and 20: British Museum; page 30: Robert Harding; page 31 (middle): Chloe Sayer.